Dedicated to my Great Grandmother, Kendall Starr,
Friends and Family.

Grieve not…
Nor speak of me
With tears…
But laugh
And talk of me
Beside you.
I loved you so…
Twas heaven
Here with you.

But what helped me through this book was what Kendall Starr said to me was " good times and bad, happy and sad.

I hope you can experience how I felt when I wrote these poems, and I hope you enjoy reading them as much as I did writing them.

Dear Reader,

      This book will help you visualize my view of the world and our surroundings. Most of my work is inspired by the people I interact with, and the places I've been. You'll read about the hardships faced by my closest friends and family members, the good times and bad, the happy moments and the sad. It is a poetic collection of my thoughts and feelings, visually portrayed through my own words, and I suspect that you will enjoy every line.

I hope you can experience how I felt when I wrote these poems, and I hope you enjoy reading them as much as I did writing them.

Thank you everyone!

Table Of Contents

A Masterpiece	Page 1
Accidental Accident	Page 2
Bees, Roses, Hornets	Page 3
Chaos	Page 4
Craziest White Girl	Page 5
Earth Through My Eyes	Page 6
Eric	Page 7
Fear and Love	Page 8
Feeling	Page 9
Goose Bumps	Page 10
Help Me	Page 11
Her Dance, His Sway	Page 12
Him	Page 13
Rise	Page 14
She and I Care For All	Page 15
Ticking Clock	Page 16
True Love	Page 17
Unimaginable Fear	Page 18
Unknown	Page 19
What Do You Call It	Page 20
What is Life	Page 21
World	Page 22
You Wouldn't Know	Page 23
Yourself	Page 24
R.I.P. Great Grandma	Page 25
Goodbye	Page 26

A Masterpiece

Tears of hatred
Smile of aggression
Bruises of love
Cuts of feeling
All of them are beautiful
A masterpiece of the perfect crime
Only for beaten, lonely, and neglected
Warm liquid spewing, dripping, running down
Big pools of worthless bodies lying all over the floor
A masterpiece of the perfect crime
Huge holes filled with knives, razors, and ropes
Bags holding breathless souls of the past
Our lost loves
Our people
Our crime

Accidental Accident

Amounts of red rushing through my mind.
Amounts of blue rushing through my grip.
Mind racing, racing quickly.
Images of what really happened.

I saw it, as did they.
Neutral to pale in matter of ten seconds.
Standing, quick slight pause, then falls.
Laying down, eyes wide open, Silence.

Pitter patter of racing legs.
Gasps, Screams, Crying.
Loud, ear piercing noises, radios.
Huge crowds, blood spewing into puddles.

Cars pulling away in fast motion.
Shots fired, screams of victims.
This little girl laying down in silence.
This mother wounded holding her shaking.

All of this chaos because of a stupid criminal.
Her life would be longer,
But her mother will always have her inside.
It was because of a "Stupid Criminal"

Bees, Roses, Hornets

Sunbeams, flowers rising.
Long grass, bears and honey.
BUGS BUGS BUGS!
Children playing, dogs barking,
I only made up the roses.

Gardens, plants, bugs, tools.
Country life, peaceful tranquil,
Children crying, tears swelling.
Large nests, beautiful flowers.
Colorful landscapes, still images.

The bees were the worst part,
I only made up the roses.
Did the hornets sting the goat too?
Loud noises of pain over and over,
Again until there isn't any more.

I only made up the roses.
Country life, peaceful tranquil.
Bees, hornets- when they attack,
You hardly notice any difference.
Nothing I ever had to go again.

Chaos

Knives, guns, killing
If it is possible, could we stop it?
Preventing danger in its tracks.

I'm half immuned, wishing to be full.
I wish and wish, but it will not come true.
I want to be like Cinderella with her Prince Charming.

But it never happens.
Death and Despair,
Fighting and Blood.

It is all Chaos.

Craziest White Girl

You're so sweet
You're so adorable
But when
It comes to emotions
You're horrible
Yet you're good
You're great
But you hate
When people get you

So you do what you do
And you lift weights
Like you're getting ready for dates
Like the ones with girls
And the ones for football games
Or wrestling meets

But it's all good
It's alright
You just gotta
Chill chill chill
As I sit here writing this for you
I hope you like it
If not I get it

I don't know you might want another
But then you might not wanna
It's all good
It's alright
I got you
And you got me
We're a team

We're like 2 peas in a pod
Or like peanut butter and jelly
We messy but we stick together
Being friends is good
Being friends is great

But don't hate on my poems
Just kidding just kidding just kidding
But yeah
I see the future
And I think you will like it
Because now that I'm here

You will have the greatest
Time in your life
Because I'm the craziest white girl
And if you don't get
What I'm saying now

How will you get anything in life
But oh well I'm here now
And I'm here to stay
If you need help
Just be like
Yoo Lindsay
What's good
I need your help

I'll be like alright I'm here
Because I'm here for you
So say now and forever
Were friends till the end
Peace

Earth Through My Eyes

Remember her scream,
The kiss he knew.
Dreams of four feet,
Beautiful young boys.
They read, play, study, sleep.
Man and woman write a song,
Cute cover commit to live.
Hand to pull, miles you create.
It's the important story of life.
He, She form our years to come.

Eric

My heart is a rose
Keep it warm, and nice and close to your heart.
But beware if you sturn me wrong it will prick you hard and shed your blood,
As if you were holding broken glass,
From a shattered window from me running through it from my sadness <3

Fear and Love

Fear and Love

The Frantic chill you get up and down your spine.

Cold, cautious, envy of silence.

Your alone, you and darkness that is all.

The feeling of pain, and sorrow.

Your alone, you and darkness that is all.

The loss of hope, cheer, and laughter,
I sit here with negativity and guilt.

Thinking and crying "I can't, I'm to scared"
Hitting the floor saying "I'm worthless, no one cares"
Everyone is right "I'm stupid, I shouldn't be here"

I'm alone, only with darkness nobody else.

I'm done, all fed up, in the corner waiting, waiting.

My ghostly white figure watching over my family,
Just floating here watching them laugh.

My own family laugh at my corpse, laying like I'm sleeping.
They think it is a joke, but they don't know I'm gone.

Death and Despair strain to keep from frowning they know,
They know, they are the only ones.
They were the reason, the reason I'm a cold, lifeless corpse.
I lay on my bed, my brothers know, they know,
They would have to live with this "Forever"
I warned them, many times, but they never listened.
They are scared, they are the real Death and Despair.

Feeling

How can I see
When your not here to guide me
In my heart in my soul...
The dreams of your body that I can hold...
This feeling I have I can't control...
I'm not sure if it's good nor bad...
If it's the feeling that I want...
Tell me...
Tell me now...
Because what I'm feeling is extraordinary...
And I need to know...
Is it real...
Or is it fake...
What am I going through...
Can you tell me please...
Because for some reason...
I'm weak in my knees...
For the feeling I get...
When your face is in my dreams...

Goose Bumps

With every kiss,
With every touch.

Goosebumps arise,
Goosebumps arise.

Arising from my soul,
I get that feeling of warmth.

Warmth of being needed,
Wanted and loved.

I get lost with every kiss,
Along with every touch.

I get swept away with the trance of lust,
But in the end it's always love.

My love for him,
Is and will always last.

For he has touched my heart,
And imprinted his love on me.

The way he looks at me,
His smile,
His eyes.

He is my perfect dream come true.
He is mine, forever and always.

My mother was right,
Good thing I waited for high school.

I found my one.

Help Me

If only you really know how I feel you would stop this insanity
Yet you don't and it makes me feel like I'm invisible and a joke to you
If only if only but you stay laughing, cracking, and joking around
But you don't know the pain, the sadness, torture, and guilt that I have
So as I write this, I wish you will understand, of all the people you should
But I don't know it's a mystery sometimes and other times I just plain don't get it at all
But I do most of the time but now I don't know my head is spinning
Help me before the darkness takes me
Help me before the sadness deepens
Help me before my feelings of happiness leave
Help me grab my hand as I fall, please I don't want to lose you
Help me I need you so
Help me you're my love
Help me I'm your angel
Help me oh please
Help me OH GOD please I'm getting lost
Help me it's getting darker I need the light
Help me from my nightmare

Her Dance, His Sway

She dances her dance; she sways her own way,
She leans in, when he's looking away.
She wants him so badly,
But he's swaying further and further away.

So she dances her dance, faster and faster,
She sways her own way, in a magnificent way.
When he finally looks, he wants her so badly.
But she's going on swaying on her own far, far away.

Finally he realizes why she dances her dance,
Why she sways on her own way,
Why she leaned in while he looked away.
It was because she's in love with his dance and his sway.

So he dances his dance,
And he sways his own way to get and asks her to stay.
He asks her "Please do not go, please can you stay?"

So she nods to him yes, and they go,
Hand in hand, step by step.
Now they dance their dance, they sway their own way,
And are still together to this very day.

Him

Every time I see your face I think of us being together
Every time you smile it takes my breath away
Every hug, word, and sight of you gives me a great feeling inside
A feeling I love, but will never come true
I wish it would, but won't
You put a spell on me, and only you can take me out
Only your hugs, smiles, and words
It drives me insane, but I can control it
But when you speak to me I blush, and I get cherry red
Your gorgeous sight, it's like crossing over the heaven
When you get hurt I pray for you
The way you dress, it's beautiful
Your aura is miraculous
My love I wish I could say your name
All I can say is
I'm just a figment of your imagination
I'm invisible to you

Rise

The feelings I have right now are so great so powerful.
That if only I could do something about them I would.
But for now I'm building them up so I can start fixing them.
And making the best out of them.
They are great feelings to, and some are bad.
But oh well I'm going to start an try.
I'm going to conquer not fail.
I'm going to rise not fall.
I'm not going to let anyone down nor let them see me fail.
I'm going to be optimistic not pessimistic.
I WILL LIVE NOT DIE.
I will be great and happy.
Not sad mad or depressed.
I will be the one looking down an saying.
"Yeah that's right you said I wouldn't make it.
Well look now, I made it".
Because everyone believed in me.
I was the one who pulled through!

She and I Care For All

(Aunt Jen) Not most people have a gift of being like this
of being good poets

(Me) We're all special in our own way and no one can
take that from us

Now you tell me what you think
Because it's true we all do have this gift
All you have to do is find it and when you do enjoy it

You will love it trust me I am right now
I'm using my gift I'm making my book of poems now
I'm a beginner but I write like a pro

Ticking Clock

Tick Tock, Tick Tock
Hearts racing against the clock,
Hands spinning around and around
Numbers and dashes.

Every tick every tock,
Our life comes closer to the end.
Fight! Fight! Fight!
Stay with the light.

For if we stay with darkness,
Our light will dim.
We must conquer darkness.
We must obtain light.

For light is life,
As darkness is death.
Tick Tock, Tick Tock,
Tick Tock, Tick Tock.

Five minutes what do I do?
Hearts racing faster and faster.
Four minutes what do I do?
We're coming closer to our end.

Three minutes remain,
I'm slowly losing control of my brain.
Two minutes left to spare,
I hope you knew I really did care.

One minute now,
Holy mother of cows.
Thirty seconds to go,
I'm just going with the flow.

Ten nine eight,
Seven six five,
Four three two,
One in a half.

Goodbye, now I start my new life.
With a whole new family,
More friends to gain,
A purely cleansed soul of my own.

True Love

It is more than saying I love you.
It is more than holding hands.
It is more than sending I <3 u through text messaging.

And more than smiling at one another.

True love is being there for another,
Cherishing every moment, not wasting any of it.
No fighting, b****ing, cursing, spats, or break ups.

Unimaginable Fear

The point of failing is when just simply,
Give up, you feel you're no good for anyone.

Or anything, your all used up like a tissue for allergies.
Your feelings are no more then,
Depression, despair, useless, worthless, DEATH.

But only you would feel this,
Others feel you're different,
You're better than that,
You're great,
    Wonderful
    Amazing
    Lovely

And unique in your own way.

Yet you feel like crap and feeling this,
An anger, you slowly detoriate,
Melt down into a nasty slime and sticky like scum.

"I'm worthless, no one cares"
"They are right"

It is all done, finished,
When you leave, there is no going back,
You are on your way to NO WHERE and that is where you stay.

Just an on going road through darkness,
With creatures that you wouldn't dream of seeing,
Only in your nightmares.

My nightmares are vicious, cruel, and are unthinkable.

                My Life Is This

And this is how I feel all the time.
God, Devil, or the Grim Reaper,
They can never destroy my feelings of Regrct.

Unknown

Your face is perfect.
Your body is shaped well.
Your handwriting is perfect.
Your smile is adorable.
Your features are amazing.

Quietness, which you have is a bliss,
But sometimes you need to be a little louder.
Creativity, which you also have is wonderful.
Fashion, is great and you look dashing.

You my Love are Un-Known.

What Do You Call It

You know the feeling you get when,
That special someone.

When that someone talks to you,
Hugs you.
Smiles at you.
Laughs with you.

Then when they leave,
You get upset.

But you see them again the next day,
And the day after that.

And so on, and so forth.
That feeling is so great.

It is wonderful,
It is miraculous.

It is love, caring and happiness.

What Is Life

What is life but a sign of us being here
A significance of being good nor evil
We're here for a purpose so great
That each and everyone of us
Yes everyone has to figure out ourselves
We're all unique in our own way
Your you, and I'm me
We're us, and they're them

World

I see, you see
The grays in the sad faces
The red in the blood
The black in the horrible tragedies
Drive-by's, Bang outs, Diseases
The world
Your world
Their world
Our world

You Wouldn't Know

Oh god
I see I see

But you need
To be in my mind

To see what I mean
The confusion I have

It feels to great
That I don't know I think I need to paint

Cause if you saw what I see
Then your feelings would change

Oh buddy
I would be scared

Cause how
Would you be able

You're just too incapable
And unable

Just watch this on cable

Yourself

You are who you wanna be
And no one can take that from you
Nothing in this World can take this gift that everyone has
And if they were to do so,
Then so be it,
But they're just destroying their own world
Their own way of being
Their personality
Their pride and but of course
Their own life and throwing it away

R.I.P. Great Grandma

Swelling heart with deep thinking,
Huge frown with tears trickling.

February 28, 2011

Pain inside with hiding smiles,
Deep sleep with our memories.

March 1, 2011

Hiding sadness with sweet music,
Bad day with good people.

Missing her with a heavy goodbye,
Remembering her with a sweet hello.

A hello with my swelling heart,
Where she shall stay.

Great Grandmother Frank,
Forever in my deep swelling heart.

I love you,
We all love you.

Goodbye

Eyes burning,
Warm liquid pouring out.
Memories filling my mind.

Smiles and laughter,
Hugs and kisses,
Pain and cries.

Since her last breath,
Grieving for so long.
It has been a year since you have been gone.

Loving you dearly,
But sincerely,
Missing you really.

Wishing you were here,
You watched me grow for so long,
But now your gone.

But I can still feel you,
Sometimes I can hear you,
Most times I need you.

Everyone misses you,
I miss you,
Where are you?

Eyes closing,
Liquid stopping.
Memories fading.

Goodbye, Goodbye,
Until I see you again.
Goodbye.

www.ingramcontent.com/pod-product-compliance
Lightning Source LLC
Chambersburg PA
CBHW061316040426
42444CB00010B/2673